Mike Re
Aug. 23, 2

THE BRITISH
THEIR PSYCHOLOGY AND DESTINY

By the same author:
The Death of Merlin
Labour in History and in Modern Times
The Ninth Century and the Holy Grail
The Principle of Reincarnation
West-East, A Study in National Relationships

THE BRITISH

Character, Psychology and Destiny

W.J. Stein

With Forewords by T.H. Meyer and A.P. Shepherd

TEMPLE LODGE

Temple Lodge Publishing Ltd.
Hillside House, The Square
Forest Row, RH18 5ES

www.templelodge.com

First published by New Knowledge Books, 1958
Second edition Temple Lodge Publishing, 1990
Reprinted 2015

A CIP catalogue record for this book is available from the British Library

ISBN 978 1 906999 77 3

Cover by Morgan Creative featuring 'Joseph of Arimathea Preaching to the
Inhabitants of Britain' by William Blake (British Museum)
Typeset by DP Photosetting, Neath, West Glamorgan
Printed by 4Edge Ltd., Essex

Contents

Foreword

Today not only individuals but whole nations must learn to co-operate effectively, if the abyss of destructive nationalism is to be avoided. Current international relations between the various nations and peoples of the world clearly show the great difficulties in bringing about such co-operation. Even on the economic level—where individual nations have contributed to what in fact has become a *world* economic flow of activity—narrowing nationalism seems hard to overcome.

As in the life of the individual, so in the lives of whole nations: when actions are meant to be really productive for oneself and for others, they must be born out of *cognition*. 'Know thyself'—thus sounded forth the ancient dictum to guide the actions of the individual. Amidst the international turmoils of today the Delphic word can be heard to resound from all sides, in its metamorphosed form, as appropriate to humanity of the twentieth century: *'Know yourselves as folk-souls!'*.

Walter Johannes Stein's little book is, despite its aphoristic character, an invaluable contribution to such a super-individual self-knowledge. The publication of this edition follows 33 years after the death of its author, at a time when the changing relations among and between Western and Eastern peoples point ever more clearly to the necessity of a true self-knowledge of the various folk-souls. May this book inspire the British and non-British alike, and encourage similar studies of other peoples and their individual folk-souls.

T.H. Meyer

Basel
March 1990

Foreword to First Edition

It gives me great pleasure to write a foreword to this book. Walter Johannes Stein was one of the most interesting personalities whom I have known. As a young man he was brought into close touch with the person and work of Rudolf Steiner and throughout his lifetime his strong intellectual faculty was united with the practice of a deep mystical meditation. This gave him a unique intuitive awareness and understanding of the spiritual realities behind the world of phenomena. In addition he possessed an almost encyclopaedic knowledge of many subjects, from mathematics, physics and economics to history, art and medicine, all of which he was able to correlate against the background of his intuitive perception.

He was best known as a lecturer, and his wide and continuous activity in this direction gave him little time for creative writing. For the last twenty years of his life he lived in London and he had a deep affection for that city and for the British people. He had long planned a work under the title of this book; but the pressure of his daily activities and his premature and sudden death prevented its completion to that perfection which he would have desired. The treatment therefore of the whole theme and of its particular aspects is somewhat aphoristic, but this treatment serves to illustrate his brilliant intuitive perception. He was not blind to the limitations of the British character, but it is obvious that he had a high conception of the destiny of the British people at their critical moment of human evolution.

This book is a tribute to his appreciation of the land of his adoption and, to those who knew him, it is a monument to his penetrative powers of spiritual perception.

A. P. Shepherd

Worcester
August, 1958

1
The People

Every human being who is born on British soil, is British. Other nations have not the same conception of citizenship and it is peculiar to the English to attach this importance to the soil. The fact that in other nations the child assumes the nationality of its parents indicates the difference in the conception of nationality.

Here we have the reason why the Commonwealth founded by Englishmen is able to embrace a population of differing origin and race. We find this conception in mythology in the form of the idea that the human soul, descending from heaven, becomes primarily a child of Mother Earth, and only secondarily a child of the human mother. In the days of our ancestors the newborn child was placed on sheaves to express this idea, and was addressed as 'Son of the Sheaves,' or 'Son of the Sceaf.'*

The English are essentially islanders. As such they have a different mental outlook, a different attitude of mind from that of members of other nations inhabiting peninsulas or continental plains. All islanders long for expansion; they are keen adventurers, seafaring people, wishing to maintain and expand their personality. Their adventurous spirit leads them out into the wide world. But this attitude is counterbalanced by love of their home. All this is typical of the English.

The use of the capital 'I' in writing might indicate a certain arrogance, when we remember that in other languages the capital letter is used only for the person who is addressed. But with the English it is quite natural to emphasise the personality in addressing somebody, and does not indicate boastfulness in the

* In the Beowulf Saga this word appears as *Scyld* and Beowulf is called the 'Heir of Scyld.' The name of Scjold who is the founder of the old Danish Scoldjung line of kings, indicates the same: and Skilring is the name of the old stock of Swedish kings, the Scylfing of Beowulf.

English mind. Ambition is not present when the Englishman writes a capital 'I'; it indicates the body, the position in space, whence his outlook has its start.

The English language confirms this fact in many directions, e.g., by the words 'everybody' or 'nobody'. The language itself proves that it is the body that is in mind, and not any pretensions of the inner being. But it would be a mistake to consider the English materialistic for this reason. It is true that the English mind looks to the material world and wishes to know as much as possible about it; through his body the Englishman knows himself to exist in that world, and he wishes to bring his weight to bear in that world. But he does this with natural and innate instinct, and without pretension. The English language does not make us feel centred at that place where we act. It indicates that we look down at our own body as at a possession. An Englishman is, however, unconscious of this fact and for this reason the spiritual side of his being remains outside his consciousness. The desire to approach it consciously as a philosopher is not present. There is the definite feeling that to be conscious of it would lead into great temptation, into pride. Therefore the English mind prefers to look at the body as from outside, and to refrain from being conscious of the self.

This is quite a different attitude from the one to be discovered in 'German Identity Philosophy'. Johann Gottlieb Fichte, the great German philosopher, was able to elaborate an 'Identity Philosophy' (that is, a philosophy dealing with ego-hood) without seeming arrogant, for he belonged to a nation which writes, not the 'I', but the 'You', with a capital letter when addressing another person.

This expresses the difference between the English and the German attitude of mind. The German mind lives consciously in the human Ego. The English mind is content to be conscious of the body and to act from the Ego by instinct; but there is no desire to make the Ego an object of research. And this gives to English spiritual life its characteristic nuance.

There is an immense difference, for example, between the philosophy of John Locke and that of Johann Gottlieb Fichte. Fichte calls the activity employed in the process of thinking *Tat-Handlung*. This word did not exist in the German language before his book appeared. Fichte invented it by putting two words together, i.e., 'deed' and 'action', thus creating a new word—

'deed-action'. He felt himself so active in thinking that one word was not sufficient to express it; he felt it essential to use two words. Nobody, except his followers when they were quoting him, has used this word again. It was coined for this one occasion, and for this one purpose, namely, to emphasise that the theory of knowledge has its starting-point in *thinking*; that there is no knowledge without the mind becoming as intensively active as is possible.

John Locke, being an Englishman, behaves entirely differently. We have to imagine him sitting in front of his fireplace in an easy chair, smoking his pipe and following with his eyes the changing forms of the smoke. In this position, not being active at all, but merely aware, he states that the human mind has no influence whatever upon thinking. We can just state what thoughts enter the mind and in what order they do so. It would, however, be quite wrong to imagine that John Locke or any other Englishman is incapable of active thinking. He is—but he has a strong dislike of becoming conscious of it. Nobody has ever expressed this attitude of mind more aptly than Goethe, in the words:

'Wie hast du's denn so weit gebracht?
Sie sagen, du habest es gut vollbracht!'
'Mein Kind! Ich hab' es gut gemacht;
Ich habe nie über das Denken gedacht.'

How did you achieve what you have achieved?
You have done well, so they say.
My child, I did well,
I have never thought about thinking.

The active element in our thinking, what we actually *do* when we are thinking, does not come into the open, does not enter into normal consciousness. Only retrospectively, by using our memory, can we become conscious of it. To do this is characteristic of German, but not of English philosophy.

Let us take an example from mathematics. We set ourselves to multiply 3627 by 8934. But suppose somebody were to ask: How have you done this? What did you do first? Why do you proceed from the right to the left? Why have you written this figure underneath this figure? We should then realise that the actual multiplying is one thing and the explanation as to how it is done, quite another. To be active in thinking is a different thing from describing the activity of thinking. Actual calculation and the capacity to explain the algorism are not at all the same. It is characteristic of the German mind to emphasise the algorism, and of the English mind to *apply* the algorism.

The English mind lives in the world in which the Ego dwells, and looks from there to the earth in order to bring itself to bear on earth, and it concedes the same to others. But like Orpheus in the Underworld, it must not look back to itself.

This is the attitude of mind which underlies the Western ideal of democracy. 'Do not make yourself too important. Live and act, but do not think too much about yourself. Express your opinion openly and do not be annoyed if others do the same. Do not interfere at all with another man's life of soul. That is his private affair; and perhaps not even that, because he might prefer not to be conscious of it.' This is the attitude which leads to the enjoyment of personal freedom in England. No uninvited psychoanalysis!

The Parliamentary system is based on this. Everybody is at liberty to express his opinion and after he has had his say he must be content to be outvoted. A man must find by empiric means how much of his own personality the society in which he is living is willing to digest. He must withdraw the rest and be content to wait for better times.

It is characteristic of the English mind to be able to emerge from this hidden sphere where Ego-hood lives, but also to withdraw again to this sphere and live there, outside of space and time, until space and time again offer the opportunity for re-emergence. It is impossible to understand the English attitude without realising that the English mind is all the time either emerging from the spiritual world in an approach to the material world, or withdrawing from the material world to a point of observation outside of space and time.

It happens occasionally that an Englishman becomes conscious of the fact that he lives in a wholly spiritual world from which he merely descends to become active in this world. Berkeley was conscious of this fact, and therefore went so far as to deny completely the existence of any material world. His philosophy afforded such ample proof that the money he offered to any body who could prove that his assertions are wrong, has never been awarded. It should still be available!

Berkeley, who was very interested in optics, turns to the eye in looking for an explanation of the world of phenomena. The eye looks at the outside world or turns inwards by living in memories. Both actions convey images which Berkeley does not consider essentially different. Both are phenomena. He states that the phenomena of images appear externally and internally; 'matter' he can nowhere discover. What we call 'material thing' is nothing that one can perceive; it is merely a notion. Berkeley's philosophy is not incorrect; it is merely incomplete. He was aware that the English mind is all the time on the way from the material world to the ideal world, the world of notions; or on the way back from the world of notions to the outside world.

We approach the outside world through the senses, through sense-perceptions. But these sense-perceptions like red, green, sweet, fragrant, remain singularities. A material thing like an apple is that red thing which is sweet when I taste it. But such a thing is not a chaotic conglomeration of sense-perceptions, because there is something which puts these singularities into proper order. What is it that crystallises the isolated sense-perceptions into the red, round, sweet apple? It is the notion 'apple'; it is something we think, but without being conscious that this centre around which the sense-perceptions crystallise into the material thing is a result of our thinking only. By remaining unaware of our thinking activity we remain unconscious of the creation of the so-called material thing.

If we wish to explain how the phenomena of the material world are created, we must not speak about senses, or the human body and its parts, because they too are material things. It is better to start from thinking, for no knowledge can appear unless thinking is put in motion. The objects to which thinking has to be applied are the perceptions which appear with the character of singularities. The theory of knowledge can only describe how, from these two elements, thinking and perception, all external and internal phenomena are derived. But the problem why this world, which is *one*, appears to us in these *two* forms, in the forms of thinking and sense-perceptions, can only be answered by placing oneself outside our ordinary physical consciousness. One must become a spectator who is awake *before* this division into the singularities of perception and the synthetic action of thinking is performed. To become conscious of this would mean to cease living merely instinctively in the spiritual world. Berkeley was not prepared to do this. If we do so, we make the discovery that the human Ego distinguishes itself from the rest of the beings of the spiritual world in that it divides the unitary world into thinking and sense-perception; or, as one would say, into *order* and *chaos*. The process of how the thinking which contains order, and the perceptions which are in a chaotic state, meet each other, is made unconscious; and only the *result* of this process, namely, the material world, enters our consciousness. To watch the creation of the material world in our consciousness would mean to lose the possibility of distinguishing our own Ego-hood from the rest of the world. It would mean the loss of personality. It was not to be expected that the English would evolve such a philosphy because it is not the English mission to lose personality but to evolve it.

There is, however, a line of possible further development which would not run counter to the natural attitude of the English mind, and that would be to evolve a second consciousness, a clairvoyant consciousness beside the normal consciousness, so that the one could preserve personality, and the other expand into the Cosmos. English mentality first touched this problem in Berkeley's philosophy, but was not destined to enter this field of evolution by the means of philosophy.

The task of English philosophy was to strengthen personality in the English evolution. But the second consciousness referred to is evolving and will evolve more and more in the English evolution. It has to develop, however, not in the field of philosophy, but in the field of the active will, in the economic field, leading to a non-selfish, a selfless economic world-organisation. For the evolution of the English it was necessary to uphold and maintain the material world, in order to evolve human personality. Eastern philosophies on the other hand, wrest the human being away from personality and the material world, in order to deny the lower and to evolve the higher self. The English mind has to evolve this selfless attitude in the field of *Economy*, not in a philosophical form. That is why the limitations of English philosophy are, at the same time, the sources of a future selfless world organisation.

Continental visitors who approach the island of England for the first time realise immediately after landing that they are entering a completely new world. They find with astonishment that there is really no difference between the first and second class compartments, except the difference in price. So too, sitting down in the breakfast-car, they realise that the food offered to them, although it seems at first to be most unusual in quantity, is not really too much. The average Middle-European is not accustomed to start his morning in such a realistic way! His breakfast is usually a much lighter meal. Nations differ very much in regard to food. In Holland, lunch is only a coffee meal; in England breakfast is already a small dinner. Why is this so?

Nature works quite differently in England and on the neighbouring Continent. Certain plants which on the Continent are small and grow very close to the soil, reach the height of shrubs in England. The leaves of some English trees, especially near the coast, are often much larger than those of similar trees on the Continent. Trees in England have a number of small branches very near the ground; but similar trees on the Continent would only branch out and have leaves at a considerable height. The fact is that the vital forces are stronger in England. This same secret of nature reveals itself in the greater capacity to stand a heavier meal, which so astonishes the stranger, and in the general manifestation of life-forces in the plant kingdom.

Even in a still more hidden world the same phenomena can be observed. It is not possible for everyone to be sufficiently attentive to the fine differentiation which takes place in thinking when we move from one part of the earth's surface to another. It is, however, very interesting to train ourselves to become more and more sensitive in this respect. Most people think that their mental life depends upon their faculties and education, upon the influences they received during childhood. But they would not admit that the immediate surroundings could influence the inner 'aspect' of their thoughts. It is, of course, easier to be conscious of the influence of nature upon the life of *feeling*. The waves of the sea, the marvellous scenery of an Alpine landscape, or the colours of the setting sun in the endless desert will certainly influence our feelings. But does a similar influence take place in relation to our thinking?

Everyone coming to England from the Continent could, by self-education, become alert to this influence. We are not, at this moment, speaking of the difference, e.g. between an Englishman and a Frenchman. We are speaking about the change which everyone can recognise in himself when he comes from the Continent to England, whatever his nationality may be. It is an influence of nature which must certainly give a definite imprint to the English mind that is permanently under this influence, but it is recognisable also to the visitor coming to England for the first time in his life. *Thoughts become more vivid in England.* They become less abstract, more image-like.

Modern life is too full of rush and hurry to realise that this vivification of thoughts takes place in England, but by turning to earlier epochs of history we find an example which illustrates this English peculiarity. I do not know if many of my readers are familiar with the legend of St Brandan. It exists only in the Latin language and is therefore probably not very widely known. St Brandan is mostly only mentioned in handbooks dealing with the development of geography, as he is considered to be one of the earliest travellers.

These handbooks state that at the end of the sixth century, St Brandan travelled from Ireland to discover new land. In fact, however, the description of his voyage is a description of the year, showing how a sensitive soul realises the influences of spring, summer, autumn, winter upon the human mind. St Brandan's voyage is not a voyage through space, but through *time*. What he describes is the result of his meditations as he lives through the festivals of the year: Easter, St John's Day, St Michael's Day and Christmas Day. But he relates his experience as a voyage across the sea, discovering island after island, and realising with astonishment that he finds himself back at the same place when the same Festival of the year approaches. St Brandan's voyage is nothing else than a breviary, but a breviary which is not a prayer book, but a guide book for the soul, passing through the complete cycle of soul-life just as the sun passes through the zodiac.

Saints who have had experience in meditation have always known that the process of nature reveals in steps which follow one another in *time*, what lives in the human soul simultaneously and in a more complicated way. For this reason it is of great help to the meditating soul to be aware of the particular soul force which responds to the forces of the four seasons. This type of meditation resulted in St Brandan's book, and by following what he says we experience the development of a faculty, which in ordinary life the human being does not possess, but which manifests in great perfection in the passage of the birds, namely, their instinctive knowledge where they have to fly when the season arrives for their migration. There is something in the atmosphere of England, increasing both northwards towards Scotland and north-westwards towards Ireland, which conveys to the human being an impression which resembles the faculties of a migratory bird. This is the source of the British desire for travel and adventure, that strange mixture of adventurous deeds and travels with very practical ends. In ancient days this was stimulated by the poetry of the bards.

The modern mind has lost its connection with nature. We do not go to sleep when the sun is setting, as the birds do, nor do we start work in the morning with the dawn. It is, of course, a great achievement of man to have become to a large extent independent of nature because this make him able both to rule nature and to educate himself. But in Britain there is something left in man's relation to Nature which is unspoiled, and which in most other places has gone for ever. This makes it possible for the British, despite all the technical devices of modern civilisation, to remain sensitive as it were through a thin skin—to their connection with the microcosmic world of nature. For this reason we find in Britain, both in great poetry and among simple folk like fishermen or shepherds, this sensitiveness to the hidden forces of nature, this awareness of a world which seems to belong only to fairy tales. In Shakespeare's *Midsummer Night's Dream* and in John Masefield's poetry this kind of sensitiveness is apparent.

2
Geological Influence

From the geological point of view the Thames Valley and the London basin are parts of the most recent deposits. Turning from there, however, we come, in all directions, to less and less recent geological formations. Wherever the archaic layers come to the surface the influence of nature on human beings seems to increase. They become more imbued with natural powers and more remote from the unrealities of modern civilisation. The British islands are not prone to earthquakes, and have remained, more or less, untouched. Along the boundaries of the archaic formations, however, a good deal of rupture has taken place. Where the old layers have cracked, the dark basalt of volcanic origin has passed through and come to the surface.

The soul of the island of Great Britain can be experienced if one goes in a small boat from Mull to the island of Iona, and from there over the turbulent sea to Staffa. It is most impressive to experience the difference of two places which are as near to each other as Staffa and Iona. Iona is a lovely island and nature here tells the same story as history. It was here that Columba lived, Columba the messenger of Christ. And his love seems to live everywhere, unextinguished. The mild air, the whole of nature, seems to be imbued with Christ's love. Only a few miles away, the wild picturesque Fingal's Cave seems to be an expression of the Pagan world. The loving kindness of the Christian world is not to be found in this scenery.

The contrast of Iona and Staffa forms an excellent example of the presence of both of these natural forces on the English islands. In Fingal's Cave the old rocks of the Tertiary epoch have broken down, and volcanic rock-formations have risen through the fissure. The basaltic rock has crystallised in hexagonal pillars. Nature built a church here—the nave formed by the cave, the floor represented by the roaring sea, the pillars built of basalt. The pointed arches are created by the deposits of the sea. Through thousands of years the sea has deposited sand-layers upon pillars built by the tremendous velocity of volcanic eruptions. Whoever approaches this nature-church and compares it with Westminster Abbey, will be astonished to realise to what high degree the style of English churches has been influenced by the natural forms of basaltic crystallisation.

There in Fingal's Cave, the storm roars; Fingal's breath, trapped in the vaults of the caves, sings his song. Fingal's Cave is the most famous in Staffa, but there are other caves too, each with its own particular melody. Those who are able to listen to nature's voice will soon hear more than the mere sound of the wind; they will recognise the voices of the dead tossing in the storm, or mourning in deep sounds. Ossian's poetry arose from here; inspiring forces which live on in English nature.

3
Customs and Habits

The bodies of the English have become strong as the result of nature and of certain habits. The great amount of salt distributed in the air gives a power of resistance to the skin. The English have been a seafaring people for centuries; and for centuries the salt-containing air has permeated their skin. Again, it is a habit of the English to toast their bread, thus making it crystalline. The per head consumption of salt and sugar is high.

It suits the English better to warm themselves more from within than from without, a fact which makes them consume a greater quantity of meat than other people. The high consumption of alcohol is due to this same cause. In recent years less alcohol has been consumed, and better heating introduced into the houses. With the building of blocks of modern flats, central heating has become more and more usual. In these modern houses there are fixed windows and no draughts. But where this international method of building has not penetrated one will still find typical English houses, with the open fireplace and sash-windows which never fit properly and so allow cold air to enter. No Englishman can live without fresh air; and fresh air means air containing a certain amount of salt.

In the train from Harwich or Dover the two world-conceptions of the Continental and English passengers confront each other. The Continental passenger takes care to close the windows in the compartment; the English passenger asks the ticket collector to provide some fresh air. The English body needs this air, this salt upon which his health depends. Gout and rheumatism are very common illnesses in England. This is quite understandable, as it is the tendency of the healthy English body to be provided with a large amount of crystalline substance. In his nourishment and his breathing-process the Englishman must have his necessary amount of salt. Just as fresh meat in order to be preserved is packed with a certain amount of salt, it is the habit of the Englishman to 'pickle' his body in order to keep in good condition.

As a reaction to this process applied to his body, his senses are more vivid than would otherwise be possible. The process of his thinking is somewhat phlegmatic, but it extends and is winged. Actions are guided more by instinctive habits, and less by argument and reason.

The English are phlegmatic by nature, not in the movements of the body, but in a certain attitude of mind. Vivid thoughts are combined with the quietness of an onlooking mind. His physical attributes make the Englishman a conqueror; but his conquests proceed in phlegmatic actions. 'Lightning war' is not his business, but deeds, following each other over a long period in inner logic and natural consequence.

England has had her revolutions, has even seen the decapitation of a king, but it was all for order's sake. And those responsible were not emotional, but Puritan-minded. It was the most Puritan movement in England that was responsible.

4
The Geographical and Historical Point of View

The climate of England is influenced essentially by the surrounding sea and the Gulf Stream. In comparison with other countries in similar latitudes, the climate is much milder and provides the moisture and temperature suitable for pasture and the special kind of grass which is so characteristic of England. The Gulf Stream influences the climate of the British Islands so greatly that the average January temperature is between 11-17° higher than that of other countries in the corresponding degree of latitude. The influence of the Gulf Stream extends also to Scandinavia, and even has an effect upon the harvest of Germany. But it is primarily England which receives its advantages, especially along the South-West coast where the flora shows the results of a most favourable climate. In South Devon, semi-tropical plants, e.g., giant ferns, osmunds, regalis, grow up to the height of 5 ft.

In the Scilly Islands daffodils, narcissi and lilies are found in abundance, besides many other beautiful trees and plants. Fuchsias, geraniums and myrtles reach a great size, and aloes, cacti and prickly pears flourish in the open. Everywhere along the South Coast of Cornwall one is reminded by climate and plants of the Italian Riviera. Even the geographical shape of Cornwall is reminiscent of the 'Italian Boot'. The Scilly Islands correspond to Sicily. Cornwall is the British Italy. At the position of Naples we find Tintagel.

From an historical point of view the legends of Merlin, the Magician, remind us of stories told in Naples about Virgil. Merlin is called a pupil of Virgil as we read in the history of the Magician Virgil. We are there told that Merlin learned from Virgil how to command the spirits, and having attained control over them, he demanded that they should cover the path along which he was walking, with salt. And they did so, in obedience to his wishes. This bewildering story connects Merlin and Virgil in a rather strange way, but there is some historical reality behind the connection. In the year 1150, a Frenchman who called himself Ludovicus came from England to visit Roger II, King of Sicily, in order to acquire from him the remains of Virgil and to carry them back to England. This request is an historical fact, confirmed by John of Salisbury in his *Policratus*, 2, 23. Roger II did not allow Ludovicus to take the remains of Virgil but made him a gift instead, namely a book containing the *Ars Notoria*. As Ludovicus had hoped to gain the power of a magician by the acquisition of Virgil's remains, the king offered him the book from which he would learn the desired knowledge.

All this happened during the reign of Stephen in England (1135-1154). In 1135. Geoffrey of Monmouth wrote in England his *Libellus Merlini* in which for the first time the story of Merlin is told at length. It seems that the journey and request of Ludovicus must have been made in connection with the renewed interest in Merlin, who up to this time was only a bard known under the name of Myrrdhin. The story of Merlin and King Arthur was arousing great interest in England at the end of the reign of Stephen and during the reign of his follower Henry II (1154-1189), who excavated the tomb of King Arthur. Again this is not a legend but an historical event, as Giraldus Cambrensis tells us that his friend the Abbot of Winchester, Henry of Blois, had been present at the time of the excavation and that he himself had seen the grave.

All this proves that there was some contact between Italy and England when the story of Merlin and Arthur was taking root and when the legends of Cornwall were arousing a greater interest among the English nobility. There is no doubt that there is some resemblance to the Italian legends in the story of Cornwall, and the legends about King Marke and Tristan are reminiscent of certain Italian romances. These were not written down, and were only collected at a later date. The Duke of Ferrara possessed some of them in his library, such as the *Cavalieri de la Tavola Vecchie*. In the Cornish stories, Merlin advises Uther Pendragon about the knowledge necessary for the foundation of a knightly order which is later known as King Arthur's Round Table, and the knights engaged in the various adventures enumerated seem to take revenge for events which took place between the people of Troy and the Greek heroes of the Trojan war. Among the population in 'Cornwales', where all these legends have their home, there are today many individuals with black hair and black eyes. This gives support to the view that in earlier epochs inhabitants of the South European peninsulas came over and brought their stories and legends with them. Spanish influence too can be traced.

Proceeding northwards along the coast we come to that part of the island which is called Wales. The word 'Welsh' corresponds to the German '*Welsch*' which there means a foreigner from France or Italy. The language still preserved in Wales, is a Celtic language akin to Gaelic and containing many words borrowed from the Latin. Wales represents an English France, just as Cornwall represents an English Italy. This is so much the case that the Welsh legends are actually French legends.

For example, the story of Perceval 'as given by Chretien de Troyes or Parzival' by Wolfram of Eschenbach are just as French as they are Welsh. Wolfram calls Parzival a Welshman. Wolfram's 'Waleis' is originally 'Valois' but is mentioned beside Norgals which is North Wales—a sign that Valois and Wales were confounded. For this reason Wolfram writes Waleis instead of Valeis. It seems that a vivid contact existed for many centuries between France and Marazion which was the harbour for the traders in tin. And from here (Cornwall) the romantic influence penetrated north into Wales.

If we travel from the French Mont St Michel to St Michael's Mount near Marazion in Cornwall we see with astonishment that even nature has done much to establish this French scenery again in England and the hand of man has merely finished it by building the castle on the top of the mount. It was here that Tristan and Isolde found their refuge and 'Isolde with the white hands', the Isolde of Brittany, seems to indicate the Continental part of the story. Detailed research would reveal that more or less every part of the English island has a parallel tradition somewhere on the Continent.

To give another example in proof of this statement, let us look for a moment at the East of England, to the district of Peter-borough. Peterborough was called Gildenburgh at the time of the foundation of towns. It received the privilege of Edgar in 927, i.e. the 'Liberty of Peterborough' which is still valid and confers upon this town a jurisdiction of its own, even in matters of the death penalty. In 680 the Pope declared that pilgrimage to Peterborough would be considered equal to pilgrimage to Rome. Near Peterborough is the Abbey of Croyland, now Crowland. It is situated in a low fen district, eight miles from Peterborough, on the river Welland. A monastery was founded here in 716 by King Aethelbald in honour of St Guthlac, who had told the king prophetically of his succession to the throne of Mercia. The king made a vow that if the Saint's word proved true, he would erect a monastery. This monastery was afterwards destroyed, but rebuilt by Abbot Turketyl who was a nephew of Alfred the Great, his father being a brother of Edward the Elder (901-925).

Turketyl, called Turkentals in Wolfram of Eschenbach's *Parzival*, is a famous personality, having been Chancellor to several English kings and having been known under the name of Lohengrin in the saga of the Holy Grail. He accompanied Aethelstan's sister to Cologne when she was to marry Henry the Fowler's son, which story is told at length in the Lohengrin poem. Turketyl, who was originally Irish, served the kings of England faithfully and finally retired as Abbot of Croyland. But the tale of this English hero is mostly considered to belong to the Lowland Countries. Everywhere where Turketyl passed on his way to Cologne, for example in Cleve and Antwerp, he is acclaimed as a local hero. Croyland, situated as it is in the fens, resembles the landscape of the Lowlands of the Continent and the traveller could well imagine himself to be not in England but in Holland. Innumerable watercourses can be found here, and from Roman times onwards attempts of drainage have been made. It is certainly not accidental that the district is still called Holland. There are canals leading through the countryside which are boarded by earthwork placed at a higher level than the land. Windmills which do the necessary pumping are everywhere to be seen. In more remote times forests covered these lowlands. Wild fowl, ducks and geese, godwits, cranes, bitterns, herons, ruffs, reeves and a great many swans can still be seen, and replenish the London markets.

The history of the swans is especially connected with this

territory. In England the swan is a royal bird. The king* and the largest Trade Guilds possess all the swans. Each bird is marked with a swan mark to prove its ownership.

This institution goes back to King Aethelstan, whose Chancellor was Turketyl. Aethelstan was the founder of the English towns as commercial centres. Before his time there were only military centres. When Turketyl accompanied Eadgitha to Cologne he communicated the English Law concerning the establishment of commercial centres in the towns to Henry I of Germany. As Turketyl was known as the 'Swan Knight', the swan became connected with the biggest Trade Guilds. In England at that time these were the vintners and dyers. For that reason they share the ownership of the swans with the monarch and used to commemorate it when foreign kings came to England. It was an old custom that they should then be the guests of the Vintner Company.

The original swan mark was Turketyl's lamp. At a certain place in the Fenn, where St Mary's Church now stands in the village of Cowbitt, Turketyl lit his lamp when the Danes came to invade the country, in order to warn his fellow men to take shelter behind the walls. The picture of this lamp became the first swan mark. This swan mark has been preserved by tradition in Cowbitt. That is why Turketyl, when dying, said to his monks: 'Preserve your fire.' To him this lamp was a sign and symbol of warning to watch for all dangers. The Swan Knight was forgotten in England and became a Dutch hero. There he is known under the name of Knight Helias. But Turketyl had this name when, at the time of his arrival in Croyland, no rain fell and people were speaking about Elias having power to 'shut heaven, that it rain not in the days of their prophesy.'

This is another example of how England and the Continent are linked together by legends and by their historical background. In a certain way England is either a repetition or, as in the last example, even the archetypal origin of Continental traditions.

Can one be surprised that a nation bound so strongly to the other European nations should quite naturally feel herself involved in all European affairs? A nation which realises herself to be already bound to a wider world must penetrate this world by natural instinct.

* Written during the reign of George VI.

Let us now turn to Scotland. The people of Scotland speak the English language, but with a pronunciation more similar to Continental languages. A German would understand Scottish pronunciation more easily than English. And this related not only to the language but even to the general attitude of mind. Language and mind reveal the same peculiarities wherever a similar geological formation appears.

In Scotland we find a more mountainous country, resembling, on a smaller scale, the Alps on the Continent. But by studying the guttural sounds familiar among the Tyrolian peoples or the Swiss, we hear the same hard sounds as in the Scottish dialect. The similarity of the customs and habits of these mountain nations is not only confined to the language but also appears in their dress. Naked knees are found in Scotland as well as in the Tyrol or in Switzerland.

The inhabitants of a mountainous region have their idiosyncrasies and characteristics; and examples of all of them are to be found in Scotland. The powers of nature here have more strength than in the southern parts of the island, where the civilisation of towns has become more prominent than nature. Modern conditions too, have increased migration towards the towns, especially towards London. We see there that the population of Britain is migrating more and more towards the south; nor is it easy for the Government to shift them back by reforestation arrangements, or by provisions made for the Special Areas, etc. This was quite different in the Middle Ages. The direction of pilgrimage was then northwards, from southern areas of Europe through France, along the river Rhine through Holland, at last entering the British isles, especially Scotland, where the pilgrimage path of St James finished. An example may illustrate this.

Santiago de Compostela is a city in north-west Spain. Metal ore was found there in very early times, as early as the Megalithic culture. A long time ago Santiago was the focus of the numerous parts which were used by the metal traders. At Padron, one of the ports of Santiago, there are two great stones, known as Barca and Patron (the ship and the skipper). The legend tells us that the body of the Apostle St James, after his martyrdom in Palestine, was brought ashore at Padron for burial. This tradition was already known to Charlemagne who tried, but in vain, to discover the burial place.

The legend says that Charlemagne had a vision. St James appeared riding on horseback and, stopping his white horse in front of him, took his spear, stretching arm and spear towards the heavens. Charlemagne could see myriads of sparks bursting from the point of the spear. They assembled along the heavens as the Saint moved his arm and Charlemagne saw a path being built through the stars (the Milky Way). 'This is my way,' said the Saint. 'If you wander along it, projecting this starry way down to the earth, you will find my burial place in Spain; and when you have found it, you are to build a great church.' It is interesting to know that in the Middle Ages the Milky Way was not called by this name, but was known as St James's Way; and it seems that this legend is the origin of the later name.

Charlemagne went southwards to find the burial place of the saint, but he never succeeded. His expedition is known as his travel to Ronceval, accompanied by the twelve Paladins, champions who assumed the role of the twelve Apostles. He had to return from Ronceval leaving behind his beloved friend Roland, whose adventures have been the origin of many poems. It was not until forty years later, as the outcome of new visions, that the burial place of St James was discovered. A church was built over the relics and in the course of time the city became a centre for pilgrims. And when the Royal Family of Castille became connected by marriage with that of Burgundy, which was associated with the Cluniac monks, the site acquired international significance.

Emile Mâle, who wrote a history of art in French, has collected material showing the importance of Santiago in connection with pilgrimages. He gives a geographical description of pilgrimages starting in Santiago and leading to the north (Route de St Jacques). All the important universities of the Middle Ages like those of Orleans, Chartres, Paris, and all the important cathedrals are situated along this path of pilgrimage. It is not by chance that nearly every important town has a street named St Jacques or St James, commemorating the path taken by the pilgrims' way through the town. The main buildings of the Paris Sorbonne are still situated in the Rue Saint-Jacques. A complete geography of the pilgrimage routes shows they branched out, thus creating a true image of the Milky Way.

St James is the patron of all pilgrims who make their pilgrimage on land or sea. When the Portuguese travellers and heroes of the age of discovery went to India, St James was their patron. He appeared in their battles mounted on his white horse, still using his sparkling spear; he is thus described in the Portuguese chronicles, and also by the contemporary Arabian records. We find the pilgrimage of St James leading as far south as India, and also to the north, to a chapel situated near Edinburgh by the Rosslyn river—Rosslyn Chapel. The pilgrims of St James wore broad hats and were accustomed to turn up the brim. A shell was fixed here—the sign of pilgrimhood of St James. In the times of the Crusades the shells used for this purpose were Pecten Maximum L. (Peigne, Manteau) which were collected on the beach of Ascalon, and were placed, in those days, on the pilgrims' cloaks. Later on, Pecten Jacobaeus L. were attached to the brim of the hat. These shells were taken by the pilgrims to Scotland and were deposited at the place where their pilgrimage ended.

The visitor to Rosslyn Chapel today is told by the warden that the substance of these shells was used instead of mortar when the walls of the Chapel were built. In the Louvre in Paris, on the ground floor, there is a statue showing a pilgrim of St James, equipped with hat and shell, pouch and staff.

There are two spiritual traditions which found each other and united in Rosslyn Chapel. These two traditions appear also in the history of the Holy Grail. Both of them deal with the secrets of Christianity; but one deals with the subject from the macrocosmic point of view, the other from the microcosmic aspect.

The microcosmic aspect follows the story of Joseph of Arimathea who took away with him the Saviour's blood. Wherever the Holy Blood is worshipped, this microcosmic tradition is found. Bruges is connected with this tradition. Dietrich of Alsace received from the Patriarch in Jerusalem part of the Holy Blood and took it to Bruges, together with a book in Latin which contained the story of the Holy Grail. Chretien de Troyes received the book from Dietrich's son Philip, and based his story of the Holy Grail on this source.

The other, the macrocosmic tradition, was used as a source for another story of the Holy Grail by Wolfram of Eschenbach, who shows the connection of the Holy Grail with astrology, following the Arabic tradition. His source is Flegetanis, a word derived from the Arabic language, meaning astrologer.

That these two traditions have united in Rosslyn Chapel can be seen in the symbols there used, which indicate both paths: how man can strive to become Divine, and how the Divine became flesh. Christ as the corner stone of cosmic and human evolution is shown in the Chapel. Statues in this chapel are situated in such a way that those portraying certain events of the Old Testament are placed opposite to statues portraying events in the New Testament.

These statues are connected by garlands. If we take the Bible and read through it in the way the garland leads from one quotation to the next, we shall see that the Old Testament shows how the cosmic force, the Logos, came down to earth, step by step. Reading in the same way through the New Testament, we can see how man is taken back to heaven, again, step by step. The corresponding stages of the way down and the way up are placed opposite to each other in this building. The master who built the Chapel has conveyed many secrets of evolution to those who study, not only *what* is portrayed, but also *how* it is portrayed.

When William the Conqueror invaded England he had in his service many French knights, among them William St Clair. One of his descendents was Sir Henry Sinclair, first Prince of Orkney, and as such was recognised by Haakon VI, King of Norway, in 1379. He had many other titles. Two brothers. Nicole and Antonio Zene, took service under him. They were sea-faring men and made voyages of discovery for him. In 1390, they went to the Faroe Islands, in 1391 to the Shetland Islands. Henry Sinclair became Lord Shetland. In the following year the explorations were extended to Iceland and Greenland. Nicole Zene died, but Antonio continued his travels. Fishermen had told Sinclair that large land masses existed in the West. So an expedition to America was prepared and Labrador was discovered.

All this happened 100 years before Columbus, who should not be considered as the discoverer of America, but only as the publisher of an already long-known fact. And even this is only partly true, as Columbus died before realising that he had been in America and not in the West Indies.

Rosslyn Chapel is most remarkable for its architectural style. Spanish and Portuguese influences have been at work to create these architectural forms. As we know already that the pilgrims of Santiago de Compostela carried their shells to Rosslyn Chapel, we cannot be astonished to find this Spanish influence in the architecture. But there was also Portuguese influence, and through this, Indian influence. When Portugal discovered India, a new style, the style of King Manuel, evolved in Portugal connecting the Gothic style with the Indian.

This is especially true of the 'Prentice Pillar'. The master mason, having received from the Founder the model of a pillar which was thought to be the pillar of King Solomon's Temple, hesitated to carry it out until he had been to Rome to see the original, now exhibited in St Peter's and also appearing in Raphael's Cartoons in the Victoria and Albert Museum in London. But in his absence an apprentice had a vision revealing to him a style hitherto unknown. So he completed the pillar, not according to a physical model but to a spiritual experience. When the master returned he killed the apprentice with his mallet.

In the market place in Cintra where the Portuguese kings lived, there is a pillar reminiscent of the style of the Apprentice Pillar. Is it an indication of the fact that Portugal was the medium by which England became connected with India? Strangely enough, this Indian influence leads to the same spot, to Rosslyn Chapel, where the first connection of England with America was created by the Sinclairs and the Venetian brothers in their service.

East and west, north and south, Cosmos and Man had to unite. Europe had to be built up a second time in the English Islands, concentrating all ingredients of its culture in order to create the spiritual stream which penetrates the English nature in all its varied aspects.

5
Historical Position of English Culture

Nations do not all become really awake at the same point of their evolution. There are nations whose mythology is overloaded with cosmology. These nations represent the type which awakens at an early stage of evolution. Othes awake later, and evolve marked *self*-consciousness.

There is less cosmology in the ideas evolved by this second type. The Divine Beings who are worshipped by this type of culture appear more similar to human beings: the heavens are nearer to the earth. Half-Gods and Heroes play a more important part.

A third type does not evolve mythology at all. Late, and already selfconscious as they enter the stream of evolution, they replace the gods by virtues, and mythology by ideals. Nations belonging to this type turn their interest away from the cosmos and towards the earth.

These three types can be exemplified in the Indian, Greek and Roman cultures. Vedic literature contains a complete cosmology. But where the Self is mentioned, stress is laid on the Divine Self, not on the human, personal Self. Where the personal Self appears in Indian literature it is shown as belonging to the future. The teaching delivered by Krishna to his pupil Ardjuna prepares man to enter into personal evolution in a rightful way, without forgetting eternity. But when we turn to Homer we find heroes and man-like Gods, Gods who do not dwell in a high, unapproachable heaven, but quarrel mightily with each other, like human beings. It was left to the Romans to replace the Divine by abstract virtues, and here we see the members of the Senate offering incense to an abstract idea, 'Victoria'.

Considering these three steps of evolution towards the earth, there can be no doubt which type resembles the English mentality. It is the great task of our culture to unfold the self-conscious soul. Science, not mythology, is the standard around which we rally, and all our interest is dedicated to the earth. This does not mean that the English are not interested in the cosmos. This interest is present to a high degree, but the English mind tends to approach the cosmos with physical instruments and scientific theories like those of Newton, or in our time, of Jeans, or the innumerable practical astronomers.

If ancient India had known what we know today about atomic structure, this would have been taken as proof that the cosmos, with all its stars, is actually working in the physical structure of matter. But Sir James Jeans writes: 'In the universe around us the attraction between electric charges of opposite sign, positive and negative, follows, as it happens, precisely the same law as gravitation, the attraction falling off as the inverse square of the distance between two charges.

'Thus the nucleus-electron system is similar in all respects to a sun-planet system, and the orbits which an electron can describe around a central nucleus are precisely identical with those which a planet can describe about a central sun; they consist of a system of ellipses, each having the nucleus in one focus.' For the modern Englishman the discovery and understanding of the cosmos must take its course through a telluric intelligence.

The English belong to that type of people who enter late into evolution. When the English were only at the point of changing over from their tribal history to the first beginnings of states, Indians, Persians, Babylonians, Egyptians, Greeks and Romans had already reached very advanced stages of their evolution. India had a most elaborate cosmology unveiling the secrets of cosmic space. The Persians had invented the calendar and laid the foundation stone for every future chronological system. Babylon and Egypt had studied the influence of the planets upon the earth and had learnt to imprint into terrestrial measurements the law of the cosmos. The Greeks, enjoying this world to the utmost, had expressed their human feelings in wonderful art. And the Romans had secured by conquest the whole world known at that time.

All this was necessary before the English mind could evolve, emerging as it did out of the tribal movements of Germanic peoples in the epoch of the wanderings of the peoples. Representing a new cultural epoch, these peoples awakened, and among them, the English, placing themselves in a world in which the personal self needs material surroundings. This is shown in the relationship of the English to the arts.

6
English Painting

As long as painting was still an art in the service of religion the English did not feel the necessity to engage in it. Painting was influenced by Byzantine mosaics, which depict Angels and other Divine Beings appearing out of a golden background. Perspective was not yet invented and the figures were not placed into three dimensional space. As painting was supposed to represent visions, the figures in the pictures were distributed entirely in one plane and no necessity was felt to indicate perspective.

This stage of painting could not interest the English mind. There could have been no English Cimabue. For a nation whose task was to evolve personality there was no question of entering into the domain of painting at this stage of affairs. For this reason it is quite natural that the English only began to be interested in painting when personality and realism began to play an important role in the art. But even then the English felt no desire to paint themselves. At that period they invited famous foreign painters to be their guests, and so great artists like Holbein, Rubens and Van Dyck received hospitality from important personages in London.

Holbein's sketches in the Windsor Gallery are remarkable for their simplicity. Just as the English like to express themselves in as few words as possible, Holbein with a few strokes of the brush or pencil achieves great effect in his sketches. His cool objectivity earned for him the appreciation of the English.

Rubens' paintings depict the world perceived by the senses. He gained English appreciation by his brightness of colouring, breadth of touch and pictorial conception. His *Feast of Venus*, or the portrait of *Helena Fourment ready to enter the Bath* or the *Sant Il de Fonso* exemplify this.

Van Dyck deeply impressed the English mind by his conception of personality. His portraits are unique. Living amidst a super-cultivated aristocratic society, he paints the people who are the stars of this brilliant world. In the way he painted these portraits he seemed to foresee the near downfall of this world. His portrait of Charles I shows the inmost self of the king. The historical personality is absolutely lifelike. But in the look of the king there is a kind of uncertainty which conveys to the spectator a dim premonition of his approaching destiny. Van Dyck painted a world which was on the verge of experiencing personality; but it is a world tumbling towards destruction. The approaching shadow of Cromwell's epoch can already be felt.

It was the destiny of Cromwell and his epoch to hold back the evolution of art and to depose the glittering splendour which has no reality. The time had not yet arrived for the English themselves to become painters. This iconoclasm was not a disaster, it was a necessary event of their mission that no aboriginal English art, no English painting should be born at this moment, because it was not the English mission to glorify effeminate personality.

Several steps had to be undertaken in the way of conquest of this terrestrial world before an inherently English painter could be born. Not before the Bank of England was founded (1694) did this great event take place; and it was three years later when William Hogarth was born.

It was the task of reformation and puritanism to hold back the evolution of art in England until the right time. Personality, natural science, and certain material conditions had first to evolve. But when the new understanding for personality and nature had developed England produced her own artists who entered successfully into international competition with portrait and landscape painters.

7
English Music

In his whole being man responds to music: in mind, feelings and physiological rhythm. The mind responds to melody, for melody represents that part of music which is accessible to intellect. Harmony, as the resulting balance of variety, touches the feelings. Rhythm and its ceaseless forward movement stimulates the will and the movements of limbs. That is why we can say that the whole human being responds to music.

Both secular and sacred music have played an important part in originating the various stages in the evolution of music. Occidental music starts with the element of melody as the first stage of musical development both in folksong and sacred music.

This shows that occidental music approached the human being from the side of intellectuality. It took a long time before simple melody was followed by polyphonic music in which harmony was added to melody. It was among the Dutch people that this important step was taken. And it was in their folksongs that harmony was introduced into Western music. Dutchmen in the service of the Papal Court introduced this new element into church music.

The third element, rhythm, in which will-force expresses itself, passes through a twofold evolution. It lives at first in the rhythm of breathing and blood pulsation. A normal human being breathes eighteen times a minute, and the blood pulsates seventy-two times a minute. Thus the ratio of the rhythm of breathing and blood pulsation is 1:4; this is the basis of rhythm in poetry and music.

The earliest form of classical verse is based on this rhythm of breathing and blood pulsation. The name 'Hexameter' is misleading because in reality every hexameter contains not six but eight dactylic measure; but two of them are hidden, appearing in the form of metrical breaks. One of these breaks occurs in the middle, the other at the end of the hexameter. If we look in this way at the hexameter we shall easily discover that the hexameter is an image of the rhythm represented by two respirations separated from each other by the pause in the middle of the verse, each containing four blood pulsations, or measures.

Classical verse was based on quantity. Modern verse substitutes accent for quantity, thus introducing an intellectual element. Lung and heart were the originator of the rhythm of the classical epoch. By substituting accent for quantity, modern poetry has linked the intellect to this original rhythm. It was left to modern jazz music to link limbs to the rhythm, thereby introducing an a-rhythmical element into music.

What is now the position of the English in connection with the historical evolution of music? If we study this problem we discover that English music tried to harmonise these various possibilities of musical experience with each other.

The English attitude is always to modify the super-vivid rhythm of the limbs by the calmness of the mind. The head is the 'resting' pole of the human being; it is served by the movements of the limbs which carry the head, directed as it is by thoughts. It is characteristic of the English to calm the unruliness of the will-force by action of the mind; but also to stimulate the excessive phlegm of the head by means of will activity.

This is what gives to the thoughts of the English mind their vividness and their appearance of being permeated by reality. The Englishman lives between head and limbs, in breathing and blood pulsation, or, expressed in musical terms, in the sphere of harmony; there is at once a calmness and vividness, and balance between what is above and what is below.

But the Englishman does not like to show his feelings. This does not indicate lack of feeling, but means that he is conscious of the fact that feeling is confined to that part of the human being where idea and volition keep the balance. This attitude of soul made English music active in the epoch of harmony and counterpoint. In the musical creations of Purcell this stage of evolution is shown.

If this description of the English way of approaching music is true, we must expect in the future another culmination of musical art, of which symptoms are already apparent in contemporary compositions. The English mind is on the way to reaching another important stage of evolution which will be the continuation of the attitude taken hitherto.

By calming down volition, the superfluous will-force is saved, and our thinking is made vivid. But this vividness turns thinking into something new, something less abstract. Thought-conceptions are, for most people, 'brain waves', meaning that they are something more or less unreal; for they call real only what can be touched or pushed along. But thinking having been made vivid by penetration with will-force becomes a new faculty of perception, an almost clairovyant approach to living realities.

This new faculty does not evolve in the English *because* they are English, but because they are modern human beings. The whole of mankind is on the way of evolving this new perceptive thinking. It is only because the English, in an instinctive way, are so highly representative of the modern epoch, that mankind's progress appears to them as characteristic of their own natural faculty.

The force of will, however, is in danger today of slipping away from its connections with the soul, and of being dragged into the field of a-rhythmic actions and a sub-human sphere, and of becoming too closely attached to the mechanism of the limbs. A preponderance of the forces in the skeleton and the muscles threatens to make the human being brutal, animal-like, sub-human. It is continually necessary to tame this part of human nature. The brain, as the centre of consciousness, must defend itself against being overpowered by these forces. For if this happens, thinking becomes the servant alone of the animal side of man. Individualism then disappears and the person becomes a representative of all kinds of typical group life.

It is characteristic of the English mind to defeat this tendency. The English like to exercise their physical bodies. They are on all kinds of sports and admire the development of the animal part of the body but without allowing it to overpower the individual and spiritual side of the human being. It may be said that the English attitude is to develop the animal side as far as possible, but to check it just at the last moment, when control is still possible.

If a human being behaved in such a way that the animal nature were defeated utterly and from the very outset, this would create an ascetic type which is not the English nature at all. The philosopher Kant had this ideal. To him, human nature was something wrong which had to be overpowered and overruled from the brain through the conception of duty. A man should do this or that, not because he likes to do it, but because it is his duty.

This rather puritan attitude of mind is not characteristic of the English, although it played a part in a certain epoch of English history when the Puritan mentality was dominant. But we have already indicated that in this phase of history English evolution was held back for the purpose of gaining time, as certain artistic faculties were not to evolve too early, before the personal forces of the individual were mature.

Here is the interesting point where American and English psychology differ. The point at which the will-force is tamed by the action of individual intelligence, by self-education, is different in the English and in the American mind.

America is a country of immense spaces where everything, quite naturally, reaches gigantic dimensions. For this reason it was natural for the American evolution to allow for a greater proportion of untamed will-force than was ever possible for the English. But, again, because of this difference, the English and the American people are necessary complements of each other; it is essential for both of them to maintain good friendship, but it is also essential for them to uphold their standpoints, the one *vis-à-vis* the other. The difference indicated is essential for them both.

In the English nature the desire to become conscious of the unconscious part of the human soul is, by a natural evolution greater than the American equivalent. But on the other side the English mind is very anxious not to become too self-conscious. Instinct plays an important part in English modes of behaviour, as the English virtues are, in a high degree, instinctive. It is not the English way to say that a certain thing is forbidden. The English expression would be: 'It ought not to be done.' The social order is, for that reason, based on things which are 'done' and 'not done'. An Englishman is not told what he has to do, but he evolves a kind of natural taste telling him how to behave in a certain situation. This instinct which lives in the Englishman from birth, and is strengthened by education, is based on the interpenetration of the forces of the soul.

It would not be natural to an Englishman to evolve thoughts without looking immediately for their practical application. His thinking has a natural trend towards actions of the will. He has no desire to live in abstract notions. And his will-force, quite naturally, tends to make thinking more vivid and therewith thirsty for reality. For this reason it is justifiable to say that the English virtues are based on instinct.

The modern evolution of humanity, however, tends to make the sub-conscious life of soul more and more conscious. And here is the point where a great problem faces English mentality. It is a great step to learn to act consciously in a field in which, hitherto, one was accustomed to act instinctively. It is a great test for the soul. And this is the test which the English evolution has to pass. There is no doubt that it will be passed; but by undergoing this new experience, feelings, hitherto unknown, will evolve. And it is at this point that we must expect a new phase of English music.

8
Tradition in English Life

It has always been an English tradition to be conscious of England's mission, through the knowledge that the task of the English is connected with the evolution of the whole world. No chauvinistic standpoint is implied by this. It is the point of view which is natural for a people who, through past history, have become connected with a large part of the earth and find themselves responsible for a greater part of the earth's population. The form of this connection has changed in the course of history, and is still changing.

Different nations have, according to their specific psychology, different forms of connection with the trend of evolution. There are nations who look backwards, others who look forward, and some are content to live in the present. It was always characteristic of the English nation to live wholly and unrestrictedly in the present.

This does not mean that in English history and in all English life, tradition does not play a very important part. Tradition is very strong in England, but we must understand why this is so. Only a nation intensely conscious of the present, can remain unspoiled by continuing many customs, forms and manners belonging to an epoch long since passed.

On the other hand, England plans with an outlook into a wide future. Very often British policy waits and plays the spectator because the future is being considered but it is always a part of the future which is already rooting in this present life. For that reason it can be said that England lives completely in the present and is conditioned by the present.

An example of how much the past works on in life of the present day can be given by the following story. Some years ago I spent a few days in Malmesury and had a talk with the owner of the hotel where I was staying. He told me that there are one or two families resident in Malmesbury who are exempted from income tax. This was very interesting to me and I tried to find out why everybody has to pay income tax except those few families. The facts which I discovered by following up this matter are as follows: Malmesbury was the residence of King Aethelstan in the time when the Danes were making their invasions into England. It fell to Aethelstan and his Chancellor, Turketyl, to repulse the invaders. A great battle was waged. There is still a bridge called Turketyl Bridge in Malmesbury, in remembrance of Turketyl riding over it to enter the battle. The event took place a thousand years ago. But there are still a few families who are the descendants of people who took part in this very decisive battle. Aethelstan was so pleased at the victory that he promised to everyone who had taken part in this battle, exemption from all taxes for themselves and their descendants. And so today, after a thousand years, there are still a few families who have this privilege. What a country it is where a king's word after a thousand years, has a value which can be expressed in terms of money!

This example illustrates the strength of English tradition, the feeling for an eternal presence and a never-ceasing gratitude. It is characteristic of the English to live in the eternal presence. And that is why the English mission is a mission of mankind. This, without pretentiousness, is the objective reason for it. It is not the attitude of a conqueror, nor is it based on any kind of arrogance, but the English mission and Mankind's mission can be identified because of the connection with the eternal Presence.

This is the psychological explanation of why the English feel themselves responsible for the world. We have no wish to claim that everything done on the English side has originated from this ideal. We only wish to emphasise that this is the *true* form of the ideal.

9
The Ideal of Freedom

The English have a peculiar relationship to freedom. Freedom means political freedom, undisturbed use of granted rights. But is also means, as in the term Free Trade, to give everybody an equal chance. The English idea of freedom includes, to a high degree, equality and fraternity, because the freedom of one individual also means the freedom of any other. And equal opportunity in the economic field means brotherly sharing.

The ideals of the French Revolution, freedom, equality, and fraternity, seem to have originated in England and to have come to France through personalities who were engaged in the struggle for freedom in America. The fight for freedom, as understood in England, has an earth-embracing meaning and concerns every contemporary situation.

Thomas Buckle, the excellent English historian, has given convincing proof that immediately before the outbreak of the French Revolution a great number of important English people began to learn the French language and increased their travels to and in France. And especially such Englishmen who went through the fight for freedom in America began to influence France. Ideas represented by Franklin or Lafayette entered into the French Revolution, supplying ideals like freedom, equality and fraternity, and here these ideals began to take the shape of world ideals.

We can see from English history that England has several times fought for freedom. There was a fight for the freedom of the barons and the Magna Charta created the foundation of political freedom. But England also fought for religious freedom by placing herself outside the struggle of reformation and anti-reformation. In the days during which the whole of Europe was engaged in religious wars, England kept aloof. And when religion was taken as a pretext for struggle, the real issue behind it was political; the fight against world domination (Spanish Armada). To make the individual worthy of freedom, to create strong and responsible personalities, it was necessary to live through the struggles of the Puritan epoch.

The conception of freedom has not yet reached a definite form. Freedom, in its beginning, was something which concerned the individual or small groups. Then it evolved and has become a problem of mankind. To a certain extent it may be possible to forecast the future conception of freedom. Already, when speaking about music, such a forecast has been given. Thinking, feeling and will-force are about to evolve by changing the form of their interaction. This opens up new fields for our feelings, and will create, in the end, a new conception of freedom. To speak in this way is justified because what lives, half-consciously, in our volition today can tomorrow become conscious, and thus visible in the form of a concept. It is possible to forecast the future in so far as the future is already growing in us.

During the past four centuries mankind has achieved great progress in every field of science and its application. Studying this progress we can see the difference between modern times and the Middle Ages. Man has learnt to use his will-force in a very different way. The principle of experiment was known, but was formerly never used to such a degree as it has been used in the times of the growth of modern science. There is a great difference between knowing that the earth is a globe and circumnavigating the earth. Experiment has added to the world of knowledge the world of reality, of will-force.

This, in modern times, has also changed the *social* problem. In this field many experiments have been made, not all of them by the English. But the English, by remaining onlookers, have allowed these experiments to be made. Today it is quite clear that these experiments did not create forms of social life which could be considered to be ideal. Freedom is now at stake, and immediately there arises the necessity to act. This makes all the difference. As long as other people were acting, it was possible to learn as a spectator; the responsibility rested on other shoulders. Now, everything is different, because it is necessary to switch tradition and customs over into a new world which will not come of itself, which must be born out of the conception of a new ideal of freedom. Here, at this point, the English have to create a new conception of freedom, practical enough to form a new social order. It is not enough to think such a thing, or to have in mind that such a thing is necessary. Evolution has reached the stage in which it *has to be done*. New responsibility for mankind by free decision as much as by unavoidable necessity, *a new conception of freedom and its social application—these must be created by spiritual activity.*

I can see England moving into the future, active and responsible, no longer content to let things go, to learn by waiting, only moving late, by instinct, as late as possible and as little as possible. I can see an immense effort to evolve, by completely free decision and immediate response, the new faculties which are demanded by the necessities of the world today.

10
Religious Life and Aims

In England there has always been a great interest in the Bible. It is not only the New Testament which arouses this interest—it would be quite natural for a Christian nation to be interested in the New Testament—but the Old Testament as well is deeply studied. People who otherwise have little scientific or other knowledge often evince a thorough knowledge of the Old and New Testaments. Much more knowledge in this direction is found in England than on the Continent and there must be a reason for this.

The Hebrew people of the Old Testament were different from other people in many directions. They studied their own history with astonishing thoroughness; their culture was an offspring of the Babylonian culture. This people originated in a milieu in which the astrological point of view was dominant. Ancient Babylon was more interested in the heavens than in the earth. Mathematical and astronomical knolwedge had evolved to a very high degree in Babylon and we can find the continuation of Babylonian knowledge right up to the most recent times. In the Germanic Museum in Nuremberg, the famous globe constructed by Martin Beheim is exhibited. This globe shows both the starry heavens and the earth's surface, drawn on one plane. But the way in which the projection of the stars is accomplished still shows the Babylonian influence.

It was from this world that the ancient Hebrew people originated, with a deep interest in the secrets of the starry heavens. The Rabbinic legend says that Abraham's father was a general in the service of King Gilgamesh in Ur. But Abraham, and with him the Hebrew world-conception, consciously turns away from the wisdom of the stars, replacing the world of the stars by the social world of human beings.

The order of the stars reappears in the Hebrew development in the order of the generations, of descendants. The mission of the Hebrew evolution was to translate the order of cosmic space into the order of the descending human generations. It is deeply impressive to see a people suddenly and consciously turning from heaven to earth. This attitude is fascinating to the English, because they feel the same necessity to turn their interest towards the earth. Their problem is to do this, not in simple repetition, as in the pre-Christian epoch, but in a new way, corresponding to the demands of the post-Christian era.

The growing interest in material evolution makes the human being withdraw from his attachment to the cosmos. The earth can only be conquered if, for a period at least, the stars fade away. This comes to pass in definite stages. In times of antiquity mythological beings were identified with certain groups of stars and constellations. This is the epoch of the wisdom of the fixed stars. The next step is to withdraw from this and to turn all interest to the planets, giving the Gods the names of planets. Zeus or Jupiter, Hermes or Mercury or the Egyptian Thoth exemplify this stage. The next step is to preserve these planetary Gods, but in such a way that it is clearly felt that they live on only in ancient tradition. Men of old could approach them but now, so it was said, the Divine Beings are nearer to the earth, in fire, air, water, earth.

Finally, in a fourth stage, all the Gods disappear. Only one remains, the God Who came down from the Heavens, Who became human. The Logos became flesh. The history of this conception of the God is the history of the change of human interest, indeed of human consciousness, which gradually descends from the crystal sphere of the fixed stars, through the planets, towards the earth. The earth surrounded by atmospheric phenomena, the voice of God sounding through thunderstorm and lightning—this marks the stage in which the Mosaic religion takes root.

Every time one of these essential steps was taken the worshippers make that part of the world a symbol which no longer lives in actual experience, but only in tradition. As geological layers reveal the out-lived life of previous geological epochs, so the various symbols remain as petrification of religious experience. When the twelvefold zodiac disappears and is no longer populated by mythological beings, the symbol of the Round Table with the twelve shewbreads appears, representing the secrets of the twelve zodiacal signs, the Cherubim.

When the Gods of the seven planets become tradition, the sevenfold candlestick is created, together with the seven lamps. And when the four elements begin to be nothing else than fire, air, water, earth, the image of the molten sea and of the oxen looking north, west, south and east, is created. The symbols of the Tabernacle and the Temple of Solomon represent the gradual descent of the Divine, from the cosmos towards the earth; it is the way from the Old Testament towards the New Testament.

The Hebrews started their wanderings from Ur in Chaldea in a milieu of elaborate wisdom concerning the stars. Abraham undertook certain journeys which were repeated later on by the whole Jewish people. They learned, for this reason to regard him as an example worthy to be followed; but they could only achieve after a long time, by education and guidance, what he had learnt by his own intuition.

If the twelve tribes are an earthly image of the Zodiac, we can interpret the stations of the Jewish wanderings as being connected with the planets. In Ur, from whence they started, the moon was worshipped. In Egypt, Hermes or Mercury was the most popular God and the Hermetic wisdom became an educational power in Jewish wisdom. During the Babylonian captivity the people became acquainted with the Goddess Istar, who is Venus. By degrees they approached the secrets connected with the sun whose symbol is wine, as an element additional to bread or manna which represents moon-worship. When Melchisedek appears with bread and wine he shows himself to be a priest of sun and moon.

Moses was able to remain the leader of the Jews up to the moment when manna was distributed, but he was not able to approach the Promised Land. The leader of this last journey was Joshua who is connected with the discovery of the Promised Land, and adds the grape, the wine, to the bread. For this reason, he is the one who has moon and sun at his command. The whole journey was accomplished when Christ appeared among the twelve Apostles, as the sun appears among the twelve Zodiacal constellations.

This projection of the whole cosmos into the terrestrial world is of the deepest interest to the English mind because the English feel, when listening to the story of the Old Testament, that it contains, in symbols, the secrets of their own soul.

When they read the Book of Genesis, Chapter 49, how Jacob called unto him his sons, he characterises each of them in such a way that it is easy for us to find their connection with the Zodiac. He calls Reuben as unstable as water because he stands for Aquarius. He enumerates Simeon and Levy together as they stand for Gemini, the Twins. Of Judah he says that he is a lion's whelp, because he stands for Leo, and so on. But the essential feature in Jewish evolution was the turning away from the visible mythological Gods who dwelt among the stars, towards the invisible, One God, Who dwells in the selfless self of man. This God is *one* God because of the *one*ness of the human Ego, and that is why this God says of himself that he is the 'I am,' the principle of the Ego-hood.

The Jews went to Babylon, to Egypt and to the Promised Land because it was necessary for them to confront, in living experience, the Divine worshipped in its external and visible symbol and its other, invisible appearance, *within* the human soul. The fascination of this history is that we learn from it to be ourselves, to find inwardly in the Self, the responsibility for the whole world.

In that historical epoch in which the other nations of Europe were entangled in struggles about the various forms of Christian confessions, English history assumed a shape making it unnecessary for the English to take such an active part in the struggles of the Reformation and counter-Reformation as the rest of Europe. In the battle on the 'White Mount', 1620, the husband of the daughter of James I was beaten. He was called the 'Winter King' as he ruled for only one winter in Bohemia. This defeat was not only a defeat of the Reformation, but also of England, yet it served England best, keeping her from the struggles of religious warfare.

The divisions of Christian belief into various confessions originated in different interpretations of the Sacraments. Especially was there a division of opinion about the Last Supper, whether the Holy Communion should take place by distributing bread and wine among the believers, or by retaining the wine for the priest, distributing bread only among the believers. Mankind had again to take the step from Moses to Joshua, for Moses received manna whereas Joshua added the grape, the wine. It is a Grace of God not to have been drawn into this struggle, because how could one fight over the symbols expressing the creation of community! This Grace, in having been kept outside this struggle, is characteristic of the mission of England. And in times to come, England will have to fulfil a great service to mankind in connection with this secret of building a community of mankind worthy of Christ.

Many believe that people in our present epoch take no interest in dogmatic interpretations, and would, for that reason in connection with the Holy Mass, see no great difference between the Sacrament being given in one or in both forms, as bread and wine. It would, however, be a mistake to think that this problem is of no importance for our present time. Cult and symbolism represent, by tradition, living experience which once could be achieved in direct vision. But this is only one side of their meaning. We do not only continue the past epoch in our present life, we also live towards the future. And many things which, according to general opinion, exist at present as symbols, will gain more and more reality which will also be more recognised the more we live into the future. In new forms, but not with less reality, such things as the Holy Communion will live again.

Let us try to understand this process of diminishing and again increasing spiritual life. This is an epoch in which mankind realises that the Divine no longer speaks. The voice of God, guiding from within as the voice of conscience, has become silent. Man seems to turn to ideals of gross power, because the Divine, once living in the Creation, has more and more faded away. There is no mythology of the fixed stars for us, nor planetary Gods, and the four elements are nothing else but states of aggregation. Where once the Divine ruled, physics and chemistry, mathematical calculation and formulas have taken the place of the ancient Gods. In our world, man is the crown of the Creation; and he rules and transforms the world of nature, in which man is confronted with man. It was necessary for God himself to become man; otherwise there would have been no possibility to refer to him in a world in which nothing higher than man is in existence.

This seems to be a sad world, a world of the twilight of the gods, a world in the abyss of downfall. Nevertheless, it is a world full of glory, because man will resurrect from the abyss; he will rise through all the steps he gradually lost, one after the other. He will again conquer the world of the elements, the world of the planets, and finally the world of the fixed stars. And the Gods will resurrect with him. The Divine will reappear, but only under this one condition—that Man fulfils his task, that he transforms the earth, which is the field where he must become creative, constructive. A new heaven and a new earth *will* appear, but not until resurrection has taken place in a nature void of God. And this resurrection cannot start anywhere else than in man himself. The Divine had to become flesh because in man himself the Divine must be born again. Since God has become man, it is man's task to turn his own being towards God. In St John's Gospel 10:34, Jesus says to the people: 'Is it not written in your law Ye are gods?' This is what man must understand, not in pride and overestimation of himself, but in order to realise his task. The true purpose of Christianity is to accompany the human being into the darkness of matter, where he seems to lose everything except the material. Christ by taking flesh points us, not only to wisdom, but to the material world as that which makes us conscious of our divine origin and of the possibility of achieving spiritualisation again. Other religious systems have described birth and incarnation as the originators of suffering, and have admonished their adherents to avoid birth and withdraw into the spiritual. But Christianity has admonished us not to forget our first love, which is the earth. We seek the earth before we become conscious of our human mother, and of ourself. Matter is our first mother, and even the word 'materia' is built from 'mater', mother. Christianity is the religion, is the stage of human evolution in which man must understand that his destiny is to return to the heavens, to the spiritual world; but not without taking his mother, the material world, with him. For this reason, Christianity teaches each simple man to feel responsible for the earth and even for the cosmos.

Our epoch should not really speak about the Fall, but about the Rise of Man. We stand at that point of evolution where the single individual should become conscious of his great responsibility. If we watch historical evolution in our times we can see how single persons create the destiny of millions of people, of whole nations. The happiness and distress of millions depend upon ideals which a single individual may bring to effect. There is no doubt that this importance of the single personality is characteristic of the present epoch. But what is it that is coming to the fore, born within the individual soul, and taking possession of whole nations, creating new forms of government and a new social structure? The English cannot repudiate interest in this question. We are not at the end of the sacrifices and struggles concerning this religious problem, of man's relation to the Earth. It is a problem that is worthy of resurrection within the soul of a responsible leader. It is the modern form of the problem of transubstantiation. And Britain cannot afford not to answer this question.

We are still guests at the Table of the Lord. But in our present epoch He does not dwell in churches alone; His table is the wide world. The breaking of the bread still continues; the Holy Host must be distributed. But modern man no longer calls it the Holy Host. He speaks of raw materials, of primary products, of the access to them, and the problem of their distribution.

During the Middle Ages England was saved from participation in the struggle about the Holy Host. Henry VIII prevented it. This same England did not enter into competition in painting as long as the art of painting was ecclesiastical; and she stood aside in music as long as material culture was not fully born. England was spared from taking sides in the struggle about the Holy Host as long as it was a fight amongst confessions only. But Divine Guidance spares its warriors for the right moment. Today, England appears on the battlefield of the earthly future of mankind. Christ can be recognised by his disciples from the way He is breaking the Holy Host. The armoured knight should know who alone can break the bread.

The Divine dwells in us, in our thoughts, in our sentiments, in our brain and in our heart. The alchemists of the Middle Ages spoke about the secrets of the white and the red substance. Modern science does the same. We have discovered the white substance in the brain, and the red substance in the red blood corpuscles. They represent wisdom and love. What the heart is in us, that the chalice is in the religious service.

Here we also find the white and the red substance, representing wisdom and love. The Holy Host, the white manna, is broken and distributed, because no human being can embrace the whole of wisdom alone; only the community, assisted by ideals, can achieve complete wisdom.

The evolution of mankind necessarily proceeds gradually. In an early stage it is possible to discriminate between right and wrong. But it is not enough to *know* what is right; we must *decide for* the truth, the beauty and the right in the trend of evolution. And we must even be prepared to defend it. This means that we must accept our destiny, represented in the chalice we are to finish, because that is the cup concerning which Christ asked His Father if it were possible that it might pass from Him. It is the symbol of personal obligation. But this chalice cannot pass.

The great religious problems of the past, for which battles were fought during the Middle Ages, have not ceased to be of importance, but they live on in our present epoch in a different form. They no longer are concerned with dogmatic issues, but they have become the touchstone of human personality, on which we are tested for our worth as human beings. And it is there that the English mind, submerged in this material world, must prove its readiness to fulfil a world task.

11
The Economic Task

The English mind has always felt at home in the economic sphere. As a seafaring nation, the English organised a worldwide trade at an early date. And it was not until this trade had resulted in the establishment of national wealth that they initiated an extended home industry, and became, in a natural way, the world's financial and money market.

All earlier economic theories believe that the aim they have to serve is to establish the best possible social order. Different and antagonistic as Mercantilism and the Physiocratic system were, they both agreed that it is the aim of economic theory to show the way to the most useful social order. The Mercantilists placed all their hope in the collection of large stocks of money. The Physiocrats emphasised the importance of all raw materials and their sources. The preference for money or commodities is in dispute in these two theories.

Modern experience has taught how such one-sidedness may be avoided and how to give to each of these and other points of view their rightful importance. Not in this alone do we find the sign of the great progress, that has been made, but in the fact that we know now that there is not in existence such a thing as an ideal economic order which, being once established, would continue forever to remain the best order. We know that the economic organism is a living thing, and has its own life, proceeding according to its own inherent laws; and that, for this reason, man has not only to establish order, but has continually to watch, to direct and counteract the processes and manifestations of this complicated life, in order continuously to serve the cause for which the whole process was initiated.

It is the Anglo-American mind which, for the first time in human history, has realised that social order is not a thing which can be established by the human being according to an ideal, and then remain exactly as it originated in the mind of the inaugurators. For the first time in history the inaugurators of the Declaration of Independence in 1776 realised: '. . . that whenever any form of government becomes destructive for the ends for which they originally have been created, it is the right of the people to alter or to abolish it.' What Jefferson said here about governments has become the leading idea of the whole of modern economy, which provides for continuous management, continuous correction of the natural deviations which the inherent life of economy or social order makes necessary.

According to their nature the English have always formed their economic ideas in close relation to the real necessities of the situation and were never tempted to establish unworkable ideals. That is why we find, for example, that in times of rising prices theories appear in English economic literature different from those followed in times of falling prices. It is because the reality which surrounds us demands different thoughts in different circumstances. Adam Smith evolved his theory in times of growing industrialism and the increasing division of labour, and as this epoch is not yet over, his thoughts are still of the highest importance. The social surrounding in which he was living more and more assumed the shape of complete individualisation, and for this kind of social structure he became a leading thinker. The happiness of the community appeared to him to be secured by giving the greatest freedom to the play of individual forces. His system of economy evolved in complete independence of others and was elaborated in its outline before he met the French Physiocrats. But he shared with them his belief in the need for discovering the best form of social order.

The English mind generally has not fallen a prey to this idea, but has evolved system after system, always adapting them to new circumstances and to the world's situation as a whole. That is why we find Adam Smith still correct in nearly all his statements, although his system as a system no longer covers present-day realities. Knowing his work, we can be sure that he would have been the first to take notice of changed circumstances, and would have no hesitation in adapting himself to new developments. The avoidance of dogmatism is one of the characteristic features of the English mind.

Wherever in English history a system was elaborated, the inaugurators were prepared to leave a door open for adaptation or necessary change. We find this not only in the economic field, but also in science, and not least in political life. The English Constitution does not cover all the important arrangements which still dominate the political life of Britain; there was never an attempt to live up to the very letter of the written law alone, but free space was left for innovations, which became customarily acknowledged without being taken into the written records. Thus, for example, no provision is made in the British Constitution for a Prime Minister. This does not prevent the British from having a Prime Minister acting with all power and responsibility, but he has no salary as such and his official position is only that he is someone whose precedence comes immediately after that of the Archbishop of York.

Things which are realities do not need to be defined, and indeed definition has in it something which makes realities into mere abstract ideas. In any case the English have proved able to do without the incorporation of the Prime Minister into their Constitution. This is remarkable in an epoch of dictators.

The English are afraid of too much formation. They prefer to hold fast to old customs and to see how they change as circumstances demand. This also is the reason why they do not believe in codification of the law as much as the Romans did or most Continental States do which follow the Roman law. The English prefer to have a movable, adaptable, 'customary' law.

Adam Smith was interested in the relation of man to man. Malthus studied the relation between man and commodities. His problem was how the whole earth and her raw materials can supply us with all we need, and for how long. his studies were carried out in an epoch of rapid growth of population. He believed that the number of people inhabiting the earth grows much more rapidly than the supply of raw materials, especially foodstuffs, increases. He predicted a scarcity of food and of other necessary commodities. This has not proved true. The epoch of plenty in which we live did not enter into his premises, but that does not make his work less valuable. His thoughts were not concerned with all possible events or at least he did not elaborate them equally, but he shows one of the possible trends. Wherever we search for the attempt of English thinkers to deal with this kind of problem, we shall find them employed in the study of how to act in order to control events which may, by their own inner tendencies, work against man's interest. Adam Smith believed that this control was to be expected from the impediment which one would afford to the other, if both were left without interference, and the Manchester School elaborated this idea into the Free Trade ideal. Today we can see that this control is not sufficient. In the modern economic process we find not only trade and trade competition as active forces, but also finance, which has become a power which again follows its own inherent tendencies.

We cannot blame the economic science, of bygone days for not having reckoned with this factor, because this development of finance as a separate living entity by the side of trade and commerce is quite new. When banking was still in the hands of only a few very important individuals, man could control it by his personal efforts. When, however, money became an abstract but powerful entity man was overruled by it. It was the accumulated money which used man and no longer man who used money; and with this new development the economic thoughts had to be adapted to a new factor which began to evolve an independent life in need of control. Today we have a 'managed' currency. We have equalisation funds to be used for the balance of monetary powers, which, according to their own inherent life, evolve forces overruling the interests of man.

If we study all these new developments we can see them coming from the same sources already recognised in the Declaration of Independence in 1776. More and more forces of the social organism have split away, have become independent, evolve their own laws of existence and ask us to watch and guide them. The more this development proceeds the more we see different nations adopting a different attitude towards it.

We can watch the Western countries entering into the struggle to domesticate the wild forces of the economic process by management. America did not become independent without the help of France. It was France who paid for the American Movement of Independence, giving Jefferson the opportunity to formulate his principles. It is a direct line from here to the tripartite monetary agreement. The Western countries worked together to establish the management of the separate economic forces which seem to wish to devour man.

The East is horrified by this development. Russia, for example, feels this evolution as a nightmare. Middle Europe is squeezed between the two. In the stabilisation of the Reichsmark, Dr Schact, for example, showed that Western methods are not unknown in Middle-Europe. But the methods of the Third Reich try to shift away from the Western methods and attempt to give man—and not to the individual man but to the people—independence from the overwhelming forces of 'capitalism'. This is impossible. It is not capitalism but simply modern evolution which has given birth to the necessities of facing all those powers in the economic field which have been unfolding their inherent life.

East, West and Middle Europe have to face the same problem, a problem which cannot be solved without co-operation. It will be necessary to find ways to regulate the various forces of the economic, financial and social fields which have started to evolve their inherent life. But East, West and Middle Europe attempt to do this with different psychologies, with different estimates of the values of life.

The West will not give up its high estimate of the individual. In spite of the fact that modern economic life has proved that the principle of *laissez faire* is unable to guide *economy*, the West still insists that in the cultural sphere of life the individual and his freedom must be preserved. Middle-Europe has lately turned to an exaggerated Darwinism, considering man as a pure produce of hereditary factors. But there is no doubt that modern man can see in heredity, forces which the individual can overcome by dint of education and self-education.

Up to quite recent times, continental authorities considered education as assistance given to the forces of the individual in order to overcome the more physiological part of the human nature. This was not so in antiquity as can be exemplified in the educational principles still working in the Middle Ages, when education was considered to help the hereditary forces to evolve. In the educational system of Thomas Aquinas as elaborated by his pupil, Aegidius Romanus de Colonna, the Aristotelian principles are still used.

The difference between an ancient and modern epoch of

history is precisely that today the individuality and personality have become strong enough not to need fostering by the physiological forces, and to overcome these forces. The problem of today is to understand that in different fields of life, different principles have proved useful. The economic sphere with its increasing complication has taught us to turn away from exaggerated individualism, but the cultural field, art, science, religious belief, ask for free action of the forces of the individual.

Thus we can see that the progress of experience has taught mankind one lesson in the economic field but will, as we must hope, teach another lesson in the field of science, art, culture and religion. It would mean a retrogression for centuries to lose in these spheres the freedom achieved by the Thirty Years War and later events. There is no likelihood of the English giving up the concept of freedom, which they have evolved step by step as we have shown, and which will make it possible to have a free hand to adapt our economic ideas to recent experience. If we can solve this problem, it will serve not only us, but also Middle Europe, and will release Russia from the nightmare of the capitalistic West.

What, then, is the next thing to do in the economic field?

We have already shown that in modern times more and more fields of the economic and social spheres have split away from the general trend and have evolved their own inherent life. When, for example, finance became powerful on its own, certain arrangements had to be made to control this inherent life of finance and to tame money. The creation of the monetary equalisation fund has been such a measure. Thanks to the experience of the last epoch we can say that to a high degree mankind has learnt to balance the monetary systems of different States.

But the next step in this direction, not yet taken but now due to be taken, is the creation of similar funds for the balancing of prices. Without this it will not be possible to switch back war economy to peace economy.

*War is expensive, and because war is so expensive it should not be stopped before a real aim is achieved. But it should not go on when this aim is achieved merely because no provision has been made for switching over into peace economy. There is every reason for pondering not only how to create the money to

---

* This chapter was written before the end of the Second World War.

continue a war, but also how to create the thoughts necessary for the moment when it ends.

In any case we shall have to deal with the problem of how to stabilise prices. While the war lasts, we shall have to discover how to do this at home, and when the war ends we shall have to know how to do it for the whole world. The elaboration of these thoughts is the next necessary step.

In our epoch the whole world is confronting the age of plenty. The thoughts evolved for dealing with too much of everything are not sufficiently elaborated. On the other hand, the thoughts concerning insufficiency are highly elaborated. The war makes it possible for all countries which together have much more of everything than mankind needs, to continue with the economy of scarcity. The moment peace comes, however, it will be necessary to switch over from the economy of scarcity to the economy of plenty—and this has to be prepared for.

Let me give an example of the economy of plenty. Before the war there was too much wheat in the world. Big stocks, good harvests and, as a result, low prices for the farmer, low prices for wheat. The men who produced the bread had no money with which to buy it. Therefore some of the merchants said: 'Let us burn the surplus.' There was great opposition to this. How can we burn wheat, as we already burn other commodities, as long as many are still hungry? We must find another way. Let us buy the surplus from the market, store it in times of plenty and sell it in times of scarcity. How much money would it mean for the whole world? One hundred million pounds a year. This is not too much. But who shall pay it? It is too much for the wheat producers. What would it cost in seven years? Do not answer 'seven hundred million pounds.' One cannot calculate like this because in seven years it will have cost nothing. Times of plenty and times of scarcity change with weather conditions. And for one hundred and fifty years there have never been more than four years of plenty in succession.

So if only we had an organisation to provide for this money in advance it could be done, it would not cost one penny. But there is no Bank of Mankind, no administration for lending the money just for the purpose of bringing things into order.

Nevertheless this is possible for the English and it would be very worth while. Because wheat is such a big commodity in the market, the price level of other commodities follows the price level of wheat. It would be a start not only for regulating *wheat* prices but for regulating *all* prices. It would be possible and it would be worth while!

It will be necessary in future to watch each raw material separately and all together for the purpose of holding prices within certain limits and in a certain ratio to each other, thereby stabilising the standard of life. The English who are responsible for such a great part of the earth and of mankind cannot escape from the solution of this problem. It would lead to many far-reaching results.

There is much talk about capitalism, but let us see what it means. Take the gold producers. They certainly are a good example of capitalists. The gold price is linked to the level of all other prices. If the commodity prices fall, the gold price has the tendency to rise, because where would you put your money if everything you buy diminishes in value? You put it into the eternal. value—gold. Will you conclude that the gold producers, are very happy when the farmers starve? No, because when the gold becomes too expensive the moment arrives when it will be demonetarised, and so become worthless.

For that reason there is a critical point for the interests of the gold producer, and if you can make him see this point where he will have all the world's gold—because nobody else can afford it—he will sit on the gold bag, but it will have become worthless. That is the moment to make the owner of the gold buy the surplus wheat from the market. By helping the farmer, the wheat price rises and the gold price falls under the danger level. And the marvellous thing is that it does not cost one penny in seven years.

In reality there is no 'capitalistic', there is no 'workman's' point of view. We are all the same family. The British Empire, together with America, is able to start such a thing.

The English mind does not believe in lasting and absolute solutions. It is the English way to start a thing which is workable. That is what the world would expect from us; that is what we can do in conformity with our own nature. Certain things come into being because we create them; others come into being by waiting for the trend of affairs to make them happen. The English are more inclined to wait, but when they have waited long enough, they act. The moment for action has come. We are our true selves not only in doing things; but are our true selves also by waiting for the right moment. We must not act alone, we must see the world's reaction. But in waiting with intelligence and reason, acting at the right moment, and then thoroughly, one is truly English.

This corresponds to the attempt to fit into our present epoch in a threefold way. It is the immediate present in which we are active but this present is also the fulfilment of a past, the reaction to it, and there is a future which will be the reaction to that moment in which we are now. This means that every moment of the present is threefold, the real present, the outcome of the past, the beginning of a far-reaching future. A man is English by virtue of living in the present but that present which is conscious of the past and responsible for the future.

England's past, of which we should be conscious, is that our roots are Roman. England and France were one country in the far past. During the Wars of the Roses, in the time of Joan of Arc, England and France were separated in order both to become helpers of one another from past to present life. England's present is her empire which is steadily transforming itself. Colonies become dominions and thus equals in the family of constitutional life which forms the crystallisation point for the agglomeration of others.

The English future is difficult to describe as it is not the English way to indulge in fantasies. But let us try.

There is an approach which withdraws from purely nationalistic point of view, which seeks to become human—human and nothing else. This is the true direction and trend of evolution. It is something that is neither national nor international, but just human; something that seems to dawn the more we try to be and to become, not only English, but Contemporaries.